THIS TRACKER BELONGS TO:

Name:

Phone:

Address:

Month: _____   **DAILY DEPRESSION TRACKER**

Day	1	2	3	4	5	6	7	8	9	10	11	12

SADNESS LEVEL

	1	2	3	4	5	6	7	8	9	10	11	12
High												
Medium												
Low												
None												

OTHER SYMPTOMS

	1	2	3	4	5	6	7	8	9	10	11	12
Fatigue												
No appetite												
Overeating												
Repeated thoughts												
Unmotivated												
Lack of Concentration												
Irritable												
Anxiety												
Isolating self from others												
Thoughts of Death-Suicide												
Feeling hopeless												
Feeling worthless												
Indecisive												

SLEEP AND WEIGHT

	1	2	3	4	5	6	7	8	9	10	11	12
Hours of Sleep												
Weight gain/Lost												

DAILY DEPRESSION TRACKER

13	14	15	16	17	18	19	20	21	22	23	24	25	26	27	28	29	30	31

SADNESS LEVEL

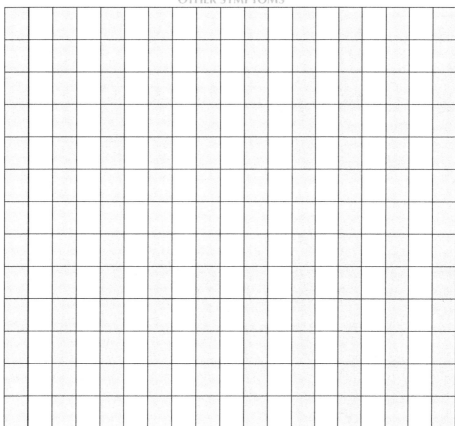

OTHER SYMPTOMS

SLEEP AND WEIGHT

Month: _____

DAILY DEPRESSION TRACKER

Day	1	2	3	4	5	6	7	8	9	10	11	12

SADNESS LEVEL

	1	2	3	4	5	6	7	8	9	10	11	12
High												
Medium												
Low												
None												

OTHER SYMPTOMS

	1	2	3	4	5	6	7	8	9	10	11	12
Fatigue												
No appetite												
Overeating												
Repeated thoughts												
Unmotivated												
Lack of Concentration												
Irritable												
Anxiety												
Isolating self from others												
Thoughts of Death-Suicide												
Feeling hopeless												
Feeling worthless												
Indecisive												

SLEEP AND WEIGHT

	1	2	3	4	5	6	7	8	9	10	11	12
Hours of Sleep												
Weight gain/Lost												

DAILY DEPRESSION TRACKER

13	14	15	16	17	18	19	20	21	22	23	24	25	26	27	28	29	30	31

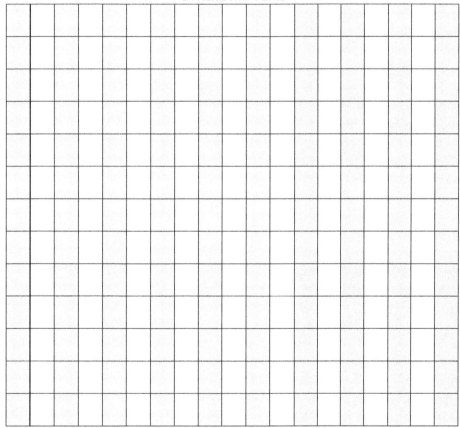

SADNESS LEVEL

OTHER SYMPTOMS

SLEEP AND WEIGHT

Month: _____   **DAILY DEPRESSION TRACKER**

Day	1	2	3	4	5	6	7	8	9	10	11	12

SADNESS LEVEL

	1	2	3	4	5	6	7	8	9	10	11	12
High												
Medium												
Low												
None												

OTHER SYMPTOMS

	1	2	3	4	5	6	7	8	9	10	11	12
Fatigue												
No appetite												
Overeating												
Repeated thoughts												
Unmotivated												
Lack of Concentration												
Irritable												
Anxiety												
Isolating self from others												
Thoughts of Death-Suicide												
Feeling hopeless												
Feeling worthless												
Indecisive												

SLEEP AND WEIGHT

	1	2	3	4	5	6	7	8	9	10	11	12
Hours of Sleep												
Weight gain/Lost												

DAILY DEPRESSION TRACKER

13	14	15	16	17	18	19	20	21	22	23	24	25	26	27	28	29	30	31

SADNESS LEVEL

OTHER SYMPTOMS

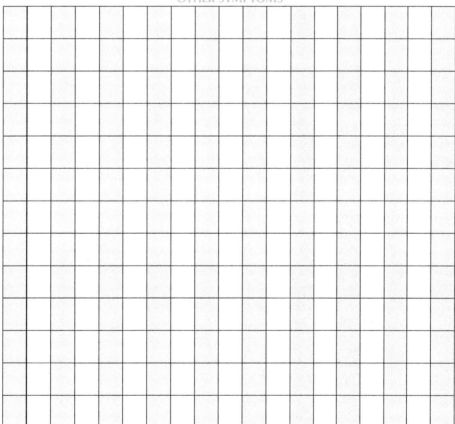

SLEEP AND WEIGHT

Month: _____ # DAILY DEPRESSION TRACKER

Day	1	2	3	4	5	6	7	8	9	10	11	12

SADNESS LEVEL

	1	2	3	4	5	6	7	8	9	10	11	12
High												
Medium												
Low												
None												

OTHER SYMPTOMS

	1	2	3	4	5	6	7	8	9	10	11	12
Fatigue												
No appetite												
Overeating												
Repeated thoughts												
Unmotivated												
Lack of Concentration												
Irritable												
Anxiety												
Isolating self from others												
Thoughts of Death-Suicide												
Feeling hopeless												
Feeling worthless												
Indecisive												

SLEEP AND WEIGHT

Hours of Sleep												
Weight gain/Lost												

DAILY DEPRESSION TRACKER

13	14	15	16	17	18	19	20	21	22	23	24	25	26	27	28	29	30	31

SADNESS LEVEL

OTHER SYMPTOMS

SLEEP AND WEIGHT

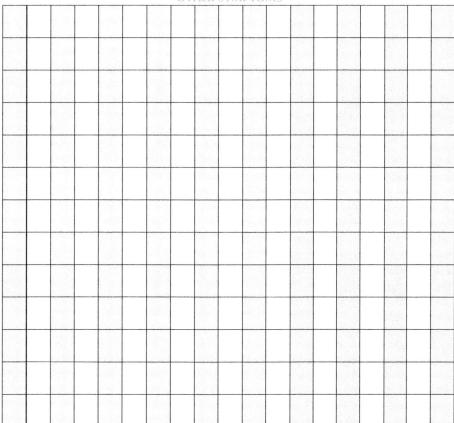

Month: _____ ## DAILY DEPRESSION TRACKER

Day	1	2	3	4	5	6	7	8	9	10	11	12

SADNESS LEVEL

	1	2	3	4	5	6	7	8	9	10	11	12
High												
Medium												
Low												
None												

OTHER SYMPTOMS

	1	2	3	4	5	6	7	8	9	10	11	12
Fatigue												
No appetite												
Overeating												
Repeated thoughts												
Unmotivated												
Lack of Concentration												
Irritable												
Anxiety												
Isolating self from others												
Thoughts of Death-Suicide												
Feeling hopeless												
Feeling worthless												
Indecisive												

SLEEP AND WEIGHT

Hours of Sleep												
Weight gain/Lost												

DAILY DEPRESSION TRACKER

13	14	15	16	17	18	19	20	21	22	23	24	25	26	27	28	29	30	31

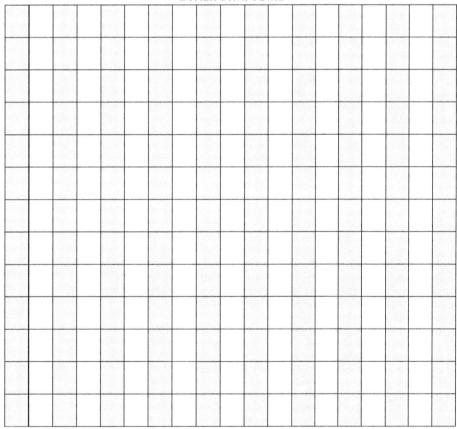

SADNESS LEVEL

OTHER SYMPTOMS

SLEEP AND WEIGHT

Month: _____

DAILY DEPRESSION TRACKER

Day	1	2	3	4	5	6	7	8	9	10	11	12

SADNESS LEVEL

	1	2	3	4	5	6	7	8	9	10	11	12
High												
Medium												
Low												
None												

OTHER SYMPTOMS

	1	2	3	4	5	6	7	8	9	10	11	12
Fatigue												
No appetite												
Overeating												
Repeated thoughts												
Unmotivated												
Lack of Concentration												
Irritable												
Anxiety												
Isolating self from others												
Thoughts of Death-Suicide												
Feeling hopeless												
Feeling worthless												
Indecisive												

SLEEP AND WEIGHT

	1	2	3	4	5	6	7	8	9	10	11	12
Hours of Sleep												
Weight gain/Lost												

DAILY DEPRESSION TRACKER

13	14	15	16	17	18	19	20	21	22	23	24	25	26	27	28	29	30	31

SADNESS LEVEL

OTHER SYMPTOMS

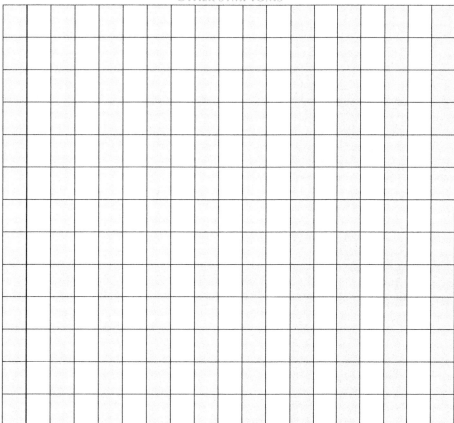

SLEEP AND WEIGHT

Month: _____   **DAILY DEPRESSION TRACKER**

Day	1	2	3	4	5	6	7	8	9	10	11	12

SADNESS LEVEL

	1	2	3	4	5	6	7	8	9	10	11	12
High												
Medium												
Low												
None												

OTHER SYMPTOMS

	1	2	3	4	5	6	7	8	9	10	11	12
Fatigue												
No appetite												
Overeating												
Repeated thoughts												
Unmotivated												
Lack of Concentration												
Irritable												
Anxiety												
Isolating self from others												
Thoughts of Death-Suicide												
Feeling hopeless												
Feeling worthless												
Indecisive												

SLEEP AND WEIGHT

	1	2	3	4	5	6	7	8	9	10	11	12
Hours of Sleep												
Weight gain/Lost												

DAILY DEPRESSION TRACKER

13	14	15	16	17	18	19	20	21	22	23	24	25	26	27	28	29	30	31

SADNESS LEVEL

OTHER SYMPTOMS

SLEEP AND WEIGHT

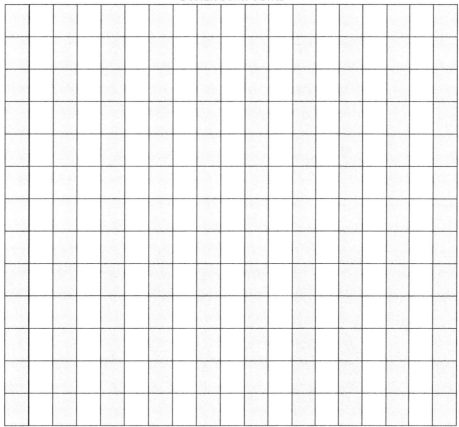

Month: _____   **DAILY DEPRESSION TRACKER**

Day	1	2	3	4	5	6	7	8	9	10	11	12

SADNESS LEVEL

	1	2	3	4	5	6	7	8	9	10	11	12
High												
Medium												
Low												
None												

OTHER SYMPTOMS

	1	2	3	4	5	6	7	8	9	10	11	12
Fatigue												
No appetite												
Overeating												
Repeated thoughts												
Unmotivated												
Lack of Concentration												
Irritable												
Anxiety												
Isolating self from others												
Thoughts of Death-Suicide												
Feeling hopeless												
Feeling worthless												
Indecisive												

SLEEP AND WEIGHT

	1	2	3	4	5	6	7	8	9	10	11	12
Hours of Sleep												
Weight gain/Lost												

DAILY DEPRESSION TRACKER

13	14	15	16	17	18	19	20	21	22	23	24	25	26	27	28	29	30	31

SADNESS LEVEL

OTHER SYMPTOMS

SLEEP AND WEIGHT

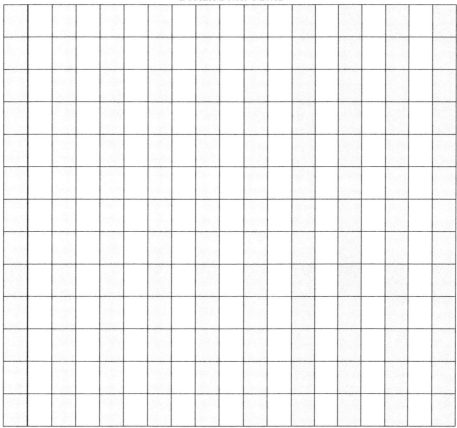

Month: _____ **DAILY DEPRESSION TRACKER**

Day	1	2	3	4	5	6	7	8	9	10	11	12

SADNESS LEVEL

	1	2	3	4	5	6	7	8	9	10	11	12
High												
Medium												
Low												
None												

OTHER SYMPTOMS

	1	2	3	4	5	6	7	8	9	10	11	12
Fatigue												
No appetite												
Overeating												
Repeated thoughts												
Unmotivated												
Lack of Concentration												
Irritable												
Anxiety												
Isolating self from others												
Thoughts of Death-Suicide												
Feeling hopeless												
Feeling worthless												
Indecisive												

SLEEP AND WEIGHT

Hours of Sleep												
Weight gain/Lost												

DAILY DEPRESSION TRACKER

13	14	15	16	17	18	19	20	21	22	23	24	25	26	27	28	29	30	31

SADNESS LEVEL

OTHER SYMPTOMS

SLEEP AND WEIGHT

Month: _____   DAILY DEPRESSION TRACKER

Day	1	2	3	4	5	6	7	8	9	10	11	12

SADNESS LEVEL

	1	2	3	4	5	6	7	8	9	10	11	12
High												
Medium												
Low												
None												

OTHER SYMPTOMS

	1	2	3	4	5	6	7	8	9	10	11	12
Fatigue												
No appetite												
Overeating												
Repeated thoughts												
Unmotivated												
Lack of Concentration												
Irritable												
Anxiety												
Isolating self from others												
Thoughts of Death-Suicide												
Feeling hopeless												
Feeling worthless												
Indecisive												

SLEEP AND WEIGHT

	1	2	3	4	5	6	7	8	9	10	11	12
Hours of Sleep												
Weight gain/Lost												

DAILY DEPRESSION TRACKER

13	14	15	16	17	18	19	20	21	22	23	24	25	26	27	28	29	30	31

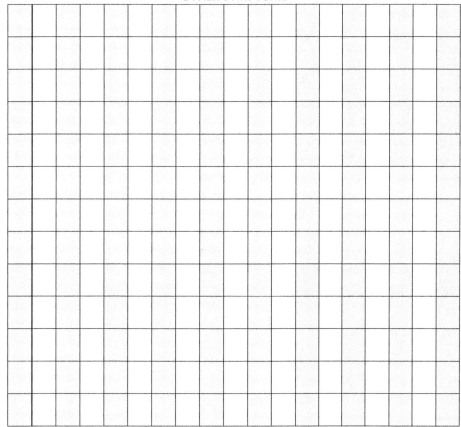

SADNESS LEVEL

OTHER SYMPTOMS

SLEEP AND WEIGHT

Month: _____   **DAILY DEPRESSION TRACKER**

Day	1	2	3	4	5	6	7	8	9	10	11	12

SADNESS LEVEL

	1	2	3	4	5	6	7	8	9	10	11	12
High												
Medium												
Low												
None												

OTHER SYMPTOMS

	1	2	3	4	5	6	7	8	9	10	11	12
Fatigue												
No appetite												
Overeating												
Repeated thoughts												
Unmotivated												
Lack of Concentration												
Irritable												
Anxiety												
Isolating self from others												
Thoughts of Death-Suicide												
Feeling hopeless												
Feeling worthless												
Indecisive												

SLEEP AND WEIGHT

	1	2	3	4	5	6	7	8	9	10	11	12
Hours of Sleep												
Weight gain/Lost												

DAILY DEPRESSION TRACKER

13	14	15	16	17	18	19	20	21	22	23	24	25	26	27	28	29	30	31

SADNESS LEVEL

OTHER SYMPTOMS

SLEEP AND WEIGHT

Month: _____ **DAILY DEPRESSION TRACKER**

Day	1	2	3	4	5	6	7	8	9	10	11	12

SADNESS LEVEL

	1	2	3	4	5	6	7	8	9	10	11	12
High												
Medium												
Low												
None												

OTHER SYMPTOMS

	1	2	3	4	5	6	7	8	9	10	11	12
Fatigue												
No appetite												
Overeating												
Repeated thoughts												
Unmotivated												
Lack of Concentration												
Irritable												
Anxiety												
Isolating self from others												
Thoughts of Death-Suicide												
Feeling hopeless												
Feeling worthless												
Indecisive												

SLEEP AND WEIGHT

	1	2	3	4	5	6	7	8	9	10	11	12
Hours of Sleep												
Weight gain/Lost												

DAILY DEPRESSION TRACKER

13	14	15	16	17	18	19	20	21	22	23	24	25	26	27	28	29	30	31

SADNESS LEVEL

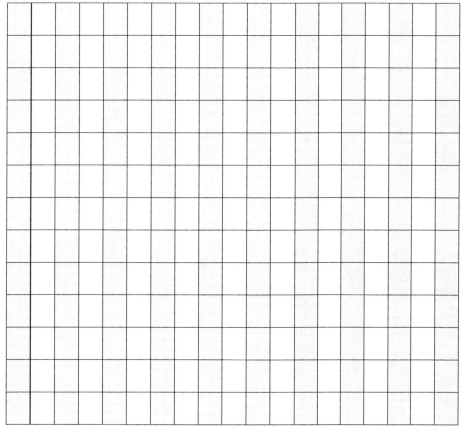

OTHER SYMPTOMS

SLEEP AND WEIGHT

Month: _____ # DAILY DEPRESSION TRACKER

Day	1	2	3	4	5	6	7	8	9	10	11	12

SADNESS LEVEL

	1	2	3	4	5	6	7	8	9	10	11	12
High												
Medium												
Low												
None												

OTHER SYMPTOMS

	1	2	3	4	5	6	7	8	9	10	11	12
Fatigue												
No appetite												
Overeating												
Repeated thoughts												
Unmotivated												
Lack of Concentration												
Irritable												
Anxiety												
Isolating self from others												
Thoughts of Death-Suicide												
Feeling hopeless												
Feeling worthless												
Indecisive												

SLEEP AND WEIGHT

	1	2	3	4	5	6	7	8	9	10	11	12
Hours of Sleep												
Weight gain/Lost												

DAILY DEPRESSION TRACKER

13	14	15	16	17	18	19	20	21	22	23	24	25	26	27	28	29	30	31

SADNESS LEVEL

OTHER SYMPTOMS

SLEEP AND WEIGHT

Month: _____ **DAILY DEPRESSION TRACKER**

Day	1	2	3	4	5	6	7	8	9	10	11	12

SADNESS LEVEL

	1	2	3	4	5	6	7	8	9	10	11	12
High												
Medium												
Low												
None												

OTHER SYMPTOMS

	1	2	3	4	5	6	7	8	9	10	11	12
Fatigue												
No appetite												
Overeating												
Repeated thoughts												
Unmotivated												
Lack of Concentration												
Irritable												
Anxiety												
Isolating self from others												
Thoughts of Death-Suicide												
Feeling hopeless												
Feeling worthless												
Indecisive												

SLEEP AND WEIGHT

	1	2	3	4	5	6	7	8	9	10	11	12
Hours of Sleep												
Weight gain/Lost												

DAILY DEPRESSION TRACKER

13	14	15	16	17	18	19	20	21	22	23	24	25	26	27	28	29	30	31

SADNESS LEVEL

OTHER SYMPTOMS

SLEEP AND WEIGHT

Month: _____   # DAILY DEPRESSION TRACKER

SADNESS LEVEL

Day	1	2	3	4	5	6	7	8	9	10	11	12
High												
Medium												
Low												
None												

OTHER SYMPTOMS

	1	2	3	4	5	6	7	8	9	10	11	12
Fatigue												
No appetite												
Overeating												
Repeated thoughts												
Unmotivated												
Lack of Concentration												
Irritable												
Anxiety												
Isolating self from others												
Thoughts of Death-Suicide												
Feeling hopeless												
Feeling worthless												
Indecisive												

SLEEP AND WEIGHT

Hours of Sleep												
Weight gain/Lost												

DAILY DEPRESSION TRACKER

13	14	15	16	17	18	19	20	21	22	23	24	25	26	27	28	29	30	31

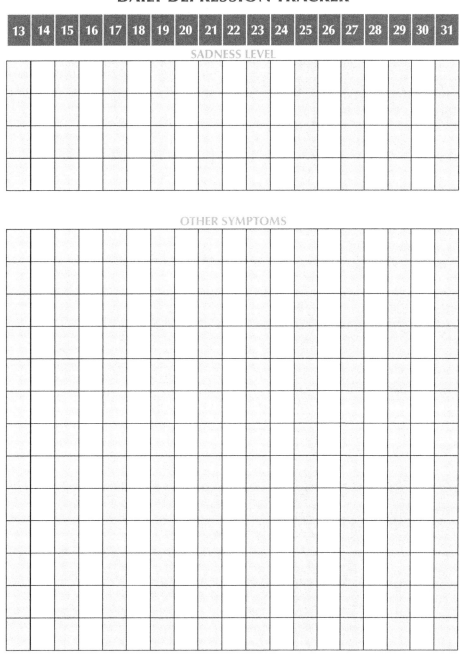

SADNESS LEVEL

OTHER SYMPTOMS

SLEEP AND WEIGHT

Month: _____   **DAILY DEPRESSION TRACKER**

Day	1	2	3	4	5	6	7	8	9	10	11	12

SADNESS LEVEL

	1	2	3	4	5	6	7	8	9	10	11	12
High												
Medium												
Low												
None												

OTHER SYMPTOMS

	1	2	3	4	5	6	7	8	9	10	11	12
Fatigue												
No appetite												
Overeating												
Repeated thoughts												
Unmotivated												
Lack of Concentration												
Irritable												
Anxiety												
Isolating self from others												
Thoughts of Death-Suicide												
Feeling hopeless												
Feeling worthless												
Indecisive												

SLEEP AND WEIGHT

	1	2	3	4	5	6	7	8	9	10	11	12
Hours of Sleep												
Weight gain/Lost												

DAILY DEPRESSION TRACKER

13	14	15	16	17	18	19	20	21	22	23	24	25	26	27	28	29	30	31

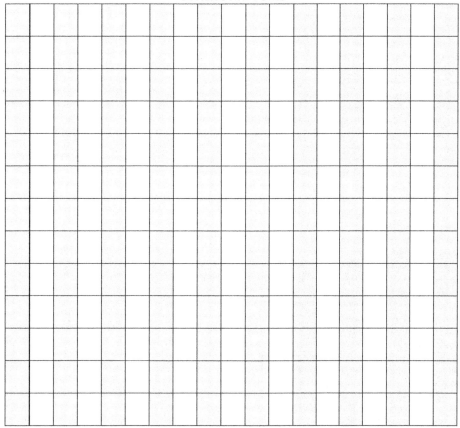

SADNESS LEVEL

OTHER SYMPTOMS

SLEEP AND WEIGHT

DAILY DEPRESSION TRACKER

Day	1	2	3	4	5	6	7	8	9	10	11	12

SADNESS LEVEL

	1	2	3	4	5	6	7	8	9	10	11	12
High												
Medium												
Low												
None												

OTHER SYMPTOMS

	1	2	3	4	5	6	7	8	9	10	11	12
Fatigue												
No appetite												
Overeating												
Repeated thoughts												
Unmotivated												
Lack of Concentration												
Irritable												
Anxiety												
Isolating self from others												
Thoughts of Death-Suicide												
Feeling hopeless												
Feeling worthless												
Indecisive												

SLEEP AND WEIGHT

Hours of Sleep												
Weight gain/Lost												

DAILY DEPRESSION TRACKER

13	14	15	16	17	18	19	20	21	22	23	24	25	26	27	28	29	30	31

SADNESS LEVEL

OTHER SYMPTOMS

SLEEP AND WEIGHT

Month: _____   **DAILY DEPRESSION TRACKER**

Day	1	2	3	4	5	6	7	8	9	10	11	12

SADNESS LEVEL

	1	2	3	4	5	6	7	8	9	10	11	12
High												
Medium												
Low												
None												

OTHER SYMPTOMS

	1	2	3	4	5	6	7	8	9	10	11	12
Fatigue												
No appetite												
Overeating												
Repeated thoughts												
Unmotivated												
Lack of Concentration												
Irritable												
Anxiety												
Isolating self from others												
Thoughts of Death-Suicide												
Feeling hopeless												
Feeling worthless												
Indecisive												

SLEEP AND WEIGHT

	1	2	3	4	5	6	7	8	9	10	11	12
Hours of Sleep												
Weight gain/Lost												

DAILY DEPRESSION TRACKER

13	14	15	16	17	18	19	20	21	22	23	24	25	26	27	28	29	30	31

SADNESS LEVEL

OTHER SYMPTOMS

SLEEP AND WEIGHT

Month: _____ **DAILY DEPRESSION TRACKER**

Day	1	2	3	4	5	6	7	8	9	10	11	12

SADNESS LEVEL

	1	2	3	4	5	6	7	8	9	10	11	12
High												
Medium												
Low												
None												

OTHER SYMPTOMS

	1	2	3	4	5	6	7	8	9	10	11	12
Fatigue												
No appetite												
Overeating												
Repeated thoughts												
Unmotivated												
Lack of Concentration												
Irritable												
Anxiety												
Isolating self from others												
Thoughts of Death-Suicide												
Feeling hopeless												
Feeling worthless												
Indecisive												

SLEEP AND WEIGHT

	1	2	3	4	5	6	7	8	9	10	11	12
Hours of Sleep												
Weight gain/Lost												

DAILY DEPRESSION TRACKER

13	14	15	16	17	18	19	20	21	22	23	24	25	26	27	28	29	30	31

SADNESS LEVEL

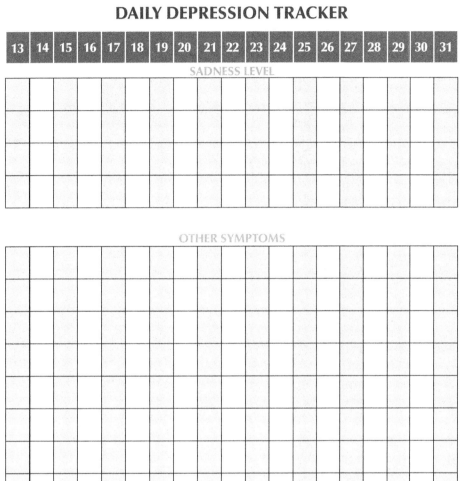

OTHER SYMPTOMS

SLEEP AND WEIGHT

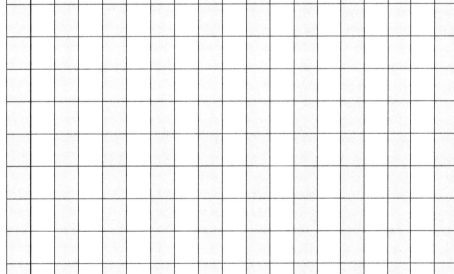

Month: _____ **DAILY DEPRESSION TRACKER**

Day	1	2	3	4	5	6	7	8	9	10	11	12

SADNESS LEVEL

	1	2	3	4	5	6	7	8	9	10	11	12
High												
Medium												
Low												
None												

OTHER SYMPTOMS

Fatigue												
No appetite												
Overeating												
Repeated thoughts												
Unmotivated												
Lack of Concentration												
Irritable												
Anxiety												
Isolating self from others												
Thoughts of Death-Suicide												
Feeling hopeless												
Feeling worthless												
Indecisive												

SLEEP AND WEIGHT

Hours of Sleep												
Weight gain/Lost												

DAILY DEPRESSION TRACKER

13	14	15	16	17	18	19	20	21	22	23	24	25	26	27	28	29	30	31

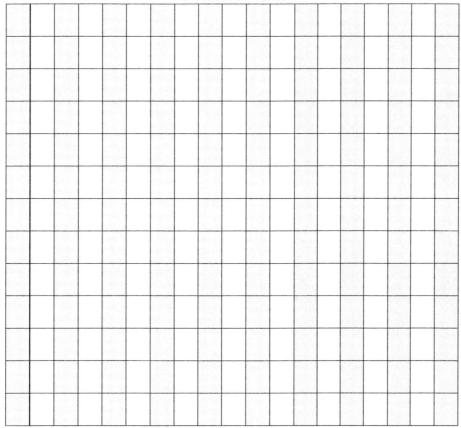

SADNESS LEVEL

OTHER SYMPTOMS

SLEEP AND WEIGHT

Month: _____   **DAILY DEPRESSION TRACKER**

Day	1	2	3	4	5	6	7	8	9	10	11	12

SADNESS LEVEL

	1	2	3	4	5	6	7	8	9	10	11	12
High												
Medium												
Low												
None												

OTHER SYMPTOMS

	1	2	3	4	5	6	7	8	9	10	11	12
Fatigue												
No appetite												
Overeating												
Repeated thoughts												
Unmotivated												
Lack of Concentration												
Irritable												
Anxiety												
Isolating self from others												
Thoughts of Death-Suicide												
Feeling hopeless												
Feeling worthless												
Indecisive												

SLEEP AND WEIGHT

Hours of Sleep												
Weight gain/Lost												

DAILY DEPRESSION TRACKER

13	14	15	16	17	18	19	20	21	22	23	24	25	26	27	28	29	30	31

SADNESS LEVEL

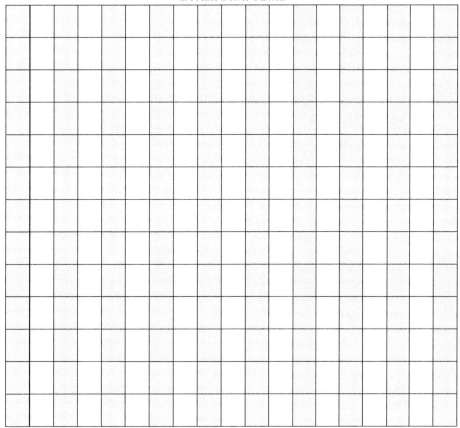

OTHER SYMPTOMS

SLEEP AND WEIGHT

Month: _____   **DAILY DEPRESSION TRACKER**

Day	1	2	3	4	5	6	7	8	9	10	11	12

SADNESS LEVEL

	1	2	3	4	5	6	7	8	9	10	11	12
High												
Medium												
Low												
None												

OTHER SYMPTOMS

	1	2	3	4	5	6	7	8	9	10	11	12
Fatigue												
No appetite												
Overeating												
Repeated thoughts												
Unmotivated												
Lack of Concentration												
Irritable												
Anxiety												
Isolating self from others												
Thoughts of Death-Suicide												
Feeling hopeless												
Feeling worthless												
Indecisive												

SLEEP AND WEIGHT

	1	2	3	4	5	6	7	8	9	10	11	12
Hours of Sleep												
Weight gain/Lost												

DAILY DEPRESSION TRACKER

13	14	15	16	17	18	19	20	21	22	23	24	25	26	27	28	29	30	31

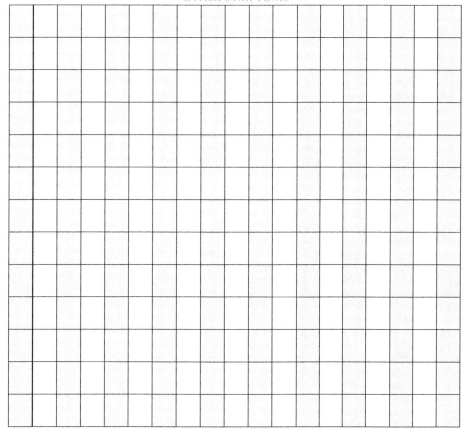

SADNESS LEVEL

OTHER SYMPTOMS

SLEEP AND WEIGHT

Month: _____   **DAILY DEPRESSION TRACKER**

Day	1	2	3	4	5	6	7	8	9	10	11	12

SADNESS LEVEL

	1	2	3	4	5	6	7	8	9	10	11	12
High												
Medium												
Low												
None												

OTHER SYMPTOMS

	1	2	3	4	5	6	7	8	9	10	11	12
Fatigue												
No appetite												
Overeating												
Repeated thoughts												
Unmotivated												
Lack of Concentration												
Irritable												
Anxiety												
Isolating self from others												
Thoughts of Death-Suicide												
Feeling hopeless												
Feeling worthless												
Indecisive												

SLEEP AND WEIGHT

	1	2	3	4	5	6	7	8	9	10	11	12
Hours of Sleep												
Weight gain/Lost												

DAILY DEPRESSION TRACKER

13	14	15	16	17	18	19	20	21	22	23	24	25	26	27	28	29	30	31

SADNESS LEVEL

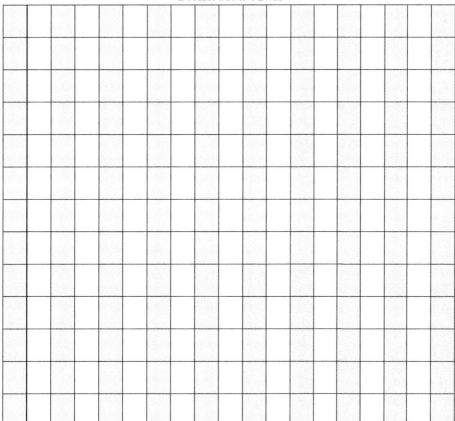

OTHER SYMPTOMS

SLEEP AND WEIGHT

Month: _____   **DAILY DEPRESSION TRACKER**

Day	1	2	3	4	5	6	7	8	9	10	11	12

SADNESS LEVEL

	1	2	3	4	5	6	7	8	9	10	11	12
High												
Medium												
Low												
None												

OTHER SYMPTOMS

	1	2	3	4	5	6	7	8	9	10	11	12
Fatigue												
No appetite												
Overeating												
Repeated thoughts												
Unmotivated												
Lack of Concentration												
Irritable												
Anxiety												
Isolating self from others												
Thoughts of Death-Suicide												
Feeling hopeless												
Feeling worthless												
Indecisive												

SLEEP AND WEIGHT

	1	2	3	4	5	6	7	8	9	10	11	12
Hours of Sleep												
Weight gain/Lost												

DAILY DEPRESSION TRACKER

13	14	15	16	17	18	19	20	21	22	23	24	25	26	27	28	29	30	31

SADNESS LEVEL

OTHER SYMPTOMS

SLEEP AND WEIGHT

Month: _____ **DAILY DEPRESSION TRACKER**

Day	1	2	3	4	5	6	7	8	9	10	11	12

SADNESS LEVEL

High												
Medium												
Low												
None												

OTHER SYMPTOMS

Fatigue												
No appetite												
Overeating												
Repeated thoughts												
Unmotivated												
Lack of Concentration												
Irritable												
Anxiety												
Isolating self from others												
Thoughts of Death-Suicide												
Feeling hopeless												
Feeling worthless												
Indecisive												

SLEEP AND WEIGHT

Hours of Sleep												
Weight gain/Lost												

DAILY DEPRESSION TRACKER

13	14	15	16	17	18	19	20	21	22	23	24	25	26	27	28	29	30	31

SADNESS LEVEL

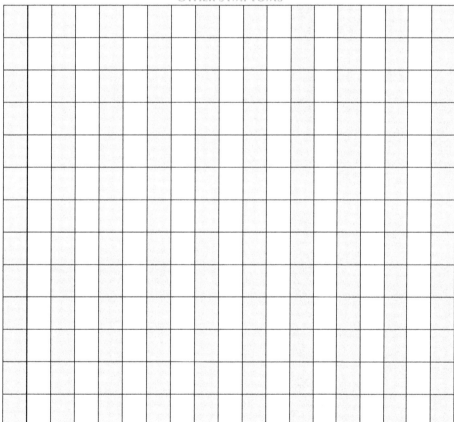

OTHER SYMPTOMS

SLEEP AND WEIGHT

Month: _____   **DAILY DEPRESSION TRACKER**

Day	1	2	3	4	5	6	7	8	9	10	11	12

SADNESS LEVEL

	1	2	3	4	5	6	7	8	9	10	11	12
High												
Medium												
Low												
None												

OTHER SYMPTOMS

	1	2	3	4	5	6	7	8	9	10	11	12
Fatigue												
No appetite												
Overeating												
Repeated thoughts												
Unmotivated												
Lack of Concentration												
Irritable												
Anxiety												
Isolating self from others												
Thoughts of Death-Suicide												
Feeling hopeless												
Feeling worthless												
Indecisive												

SLEEP AND WEIGHT

	1	2	3	4	5	6	7	8	9	10	11	12
Hours of Sleep												
Weight gain/Lost												

DAILY DEPRESSION TRACKER

13	14	15	16	17	18	19	20	21	22	23	24	25	26	27	28	29	30	31

SADNESS LEVEL

OTHER SYMPTOMS

SLEEP AND WEIGHT

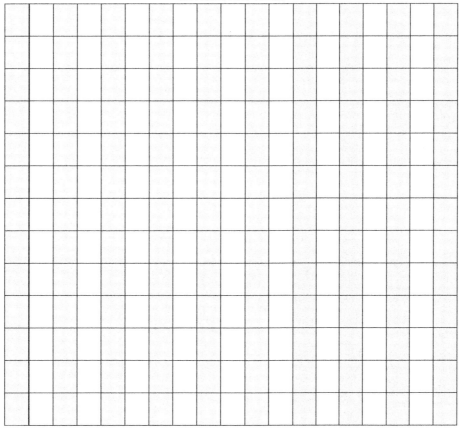

Month: _____ **DAILY DEPRESSION TRACKER**

Day	1	2	3	4	5	6	7	8	9	10	11	12

SADNESS LEVEL

	1	2	3	4	5	6	7	8	9	10	11	12
High												
Medium												
Low												
None												

OTHER SYMPTOMS

	1	2	3	4	5	6	7	8	9	10	11	12
Fatigue												
No appetite												
Overeating												
Repeated thoughts												
Unmotivated												
Lack of Concentration												
Irritable												
Anxiety												
Isolating self from others												
Thoughts of Death-Suicide												
Feeling hopeless												
Feeling worthless												
Indecisive												

SLEEP AND WEIGHT

Hours of Sleep												
Weight gain/Lost												

DAILY DEPRESSION TRACKER

13	14	15	16	17	18	19	20	21	22	23	24	25	26	27	28	29	30	31

SADNESS LEVEL

OTHER SYMPTOMS

SLEEP AND WEIGHT

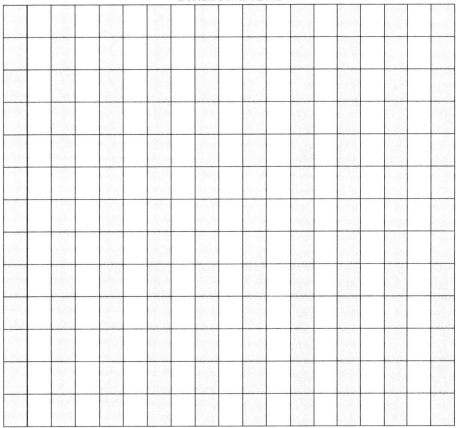

Month: _____ **DAILY DEPRESSION TRACKER**

Day	1	2	3	4	5	6	7	8	9	10	11	12

SADNESS LEVEL

	1	2	3	4	5	6	7	8	9	10	11	12
High												
Medium												
Low												
None												

OTHER SYMPTOMS

	1	2	3	4	5	6	7	8	9	10	11	12
Fatigue												
No appetite												
Overeating												
Repeated thoughts												
Unmotivated												
Lack of Concentration												
Irritable												
Anxiety												
Isolating self from others												
Thoughts of Death-Suicide												
Feeling hopeless												
Feeling worthless												
Indecisive												

SLEEP AND WEIGHT

Hours of Sleep												
Weight gain/Lost												

DAILY DEPRESSION TRACKER

13	14	15	16	17	18	19	20	21	22	23	24	25	26	27	28	29	30	31

SADNESS LEVEL

OTHER SYMPTOMS

SLEEP AND WEIGHT

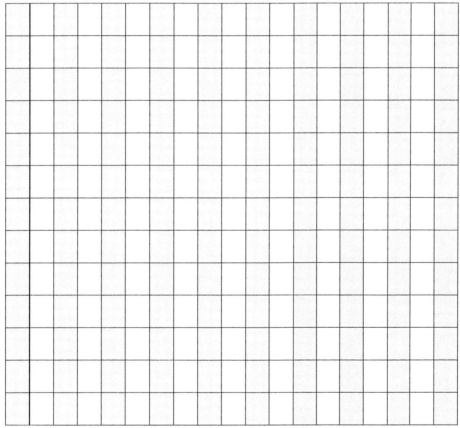

Month: _____   # DAILY DEPRESSION TRACKER

Day	1	2	3	4	5	6	7	8	9	10	11	12

SADNESS LEVEL

	1	2	3	4	5	6	7	8	9	10	11	12
High												
Medium												
Low												
None												

OTHER SYMPTOMS

	1	2	3	4	5	6	7	8	9	10	11	12
Fatigue												
No appetite												
Overeating												
Repeated thoughts												
Unmotivated												
Lack of Concentration												
Irritable												
Anxiety												
Isolating self from others												
Thoughts of Death-Suicide												
Feeling hopeless												
Feeling worthless												
Indecisive												

SLEEP AND WEIGHT

	1	2	3	4	5	6	7	8	9	10	11	12
Hours of Sleep												
Weight gain/Lost												

DAILY DEPRESSION TRACKER

13	14	15	16	17	18	19	20	21	22	23	24	25	26	27	28	29	30	31

SADNESS LEVEL

OTHER SYMPTOMS

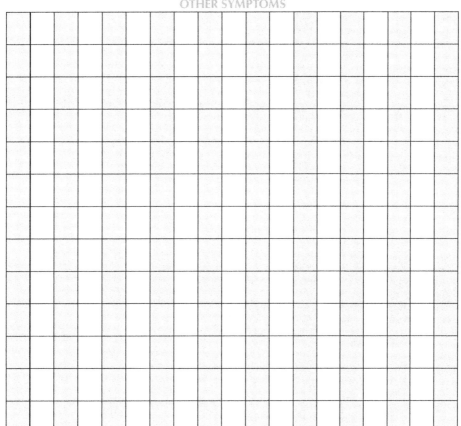

SLEEP AND WEIGHT

Month: _____ **DAILY DEPRESSION TRACKER**

Day	1	2	3	4	5	6	7	8	9	10	11	12

SADNESS LEVEL

	1	2	3	4	5	6	7	8	9	10	11	12
High												
Medium												
Low												
None												

OTHER SYMPTOMS

	1	2	3	4	5	6	7	8	9	10	11	12
Fatigue												
No appetite												
Overeating												
Repeated thoughts												
Unmotivated												
Lack of Concentration												
Irritable												
Anxiety												
Isolating self from others												
Thoughts of Death-Suicide												
Feeling hopeless												
Feeling worthless												
Indecisive												

SLEEP AND WEIGHT

	1	2	3	4	5	6	7	8	9	10	11	12
Hours of Sleep												
Weight gain/Lost												

DAILY DEPRESSION TRACKER

13	14	15	16	17	18	19	20	21	22	23	24	25	26	27	28	29	30	31

SADNESS LEVEL

OTHER SYMPTOMS

SLEEP AND WEIGHT

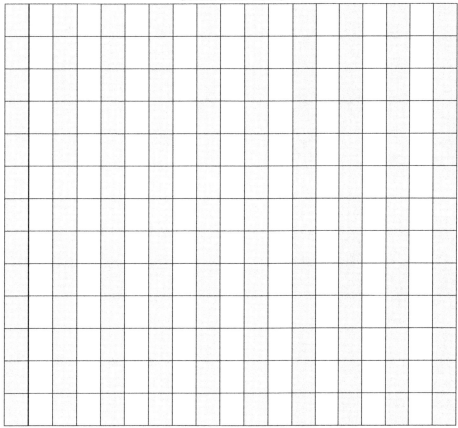

Month: _____ **DAILY DEPRESSION TRACKER**

Day	1	2	3	4	5	6	7	8	9	10	11	12

SADNESS LEVEL

	1	2	3	4	5	6	7	8	9	10	11	12
High												
Medium												
Low												
None												

OTHER SYMPTOMS

	1	2	3	4	5	6	7	8	9	10	11	12
Fatigue												
No appetite												
Overeating												
Repeated thoughts												
Unmotivated												
Lack of Concentration												
Irritable												
Anxiety												
Isolating self from others												
Thoughts of Death-Suicide												
Feeling hopeless												
Feeling worthless												
Indecisive												

SLEEP AND WEIGHT

	1	2	3	4	5	6	7	8	9	10	11	12
Hours of Sleep												
Weight gain/Lost												

DAILY DEPRESSION TRACKER

13	14	15	16	17	18	19	20	21	22	23	24	25	26	27	28	29	30	31

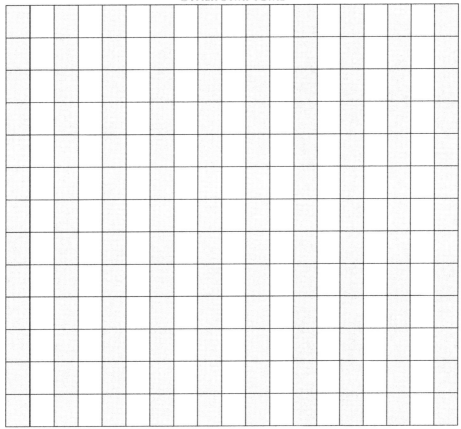

SADNESS LEVEL

OTHER SYMPTOMS

SLEEP AND WEIGHT

DAILY DEPRESSION TRACKER

Day	1	2	3	4	5	6	7	8	9	10	11	12

SADNESS LEVEL

	1	2	3	4	5	6	7	8	9	10	11	12
High												
Medium												
Low												
None												

OTHER SYMPTOMS

	1	2	3	4	5	6	7	8	9	10	11	12
Fatigue												
No appetite												
Overeating												
Repeated thoughts												
Unmotivated												
Lack of Concentration												
Irritable												
Anxiety												
Isolating self from others												
Thoughts of Death-Suicide												
Feeling hopeless												
Feeling worthless												
Indecisive												

SLEEP AND WEIGHT

	1	2	3	4	5	6	7	8	9	10	11	12
Hours of Sleep												
Weight gain/Lost												

DAILY DEPRESSION TRACKER

13	14	15	16	17	18	19	20	21	22	23	24	25	26	27	28	29	30	31

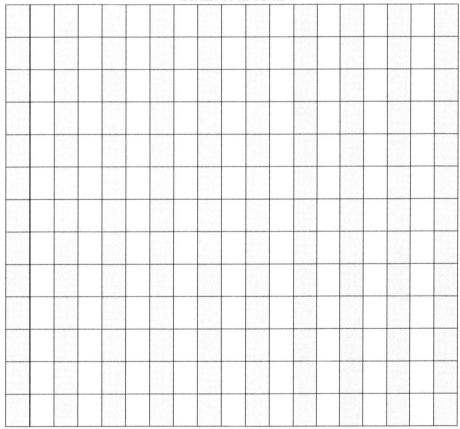

SADNESS LEVEL

OTHER SYMPTOMS

SLEEP AND WEIGHT

Month: _____   **DAILY DEPRESSION TRACKER**

Day	1	2	3	4	5	6	7	8	9	10	11	12

SADNESS LEVEL

	1	2	3	4	5	6	7	8	9	10	11	12
High												
Medium												
Low												
None												

OTHER SYMPTOMS

	1	2	3	4	5	6	7	8	9	10	11	12
Fatigue												
No appetite												
Overeating												
Repeated thoughts												
Unmotivated												
Lack of Concentration												
Irritable												
Anxiety												
Isolating self from others												
Thoughts of Death-Suicide												
Feeling hopeless												
Feeling worthless												
Indecisive												

SLEEP AND WEIGHT

	1	2	3	4	5	6	7	8	9	10	11	12
Hours of Sleep												
Weight gain/Lost												

DAILY DEPRESSION TRACKER

13	14	15	16	17	18	19	20	21	22	23	24	25	26	27	28	29	30	31

SADNESS LEVEL

OTHER SYMPTOMS

SLEEP AND WEIGHT

Month: _____   **DAILY DEPRESSION TRACKER**

Day	1	2	3	4	5	6	7	8	9	10	11	12

SADNESS LEVEL

	1	2	3	4	5	6	7	8	9	10	11	12
High												
Medium												
Low												
None												

OTHER SYMPTOMS

	1	2	3	4	5	6	7	8	9	10	11	12
Fatigue												
No appetite												
Overeating												
Repeated thoughts												
Unmotivated												
Lack of Concentration												
Irritable												
Anxiety												
Isolating self from others												
Thoughts of Death-Suicide												
Feeling hopeless												
Feeling worthless												
Indecisive												

SLEEP AND WEIGHT

	1	2	3	4	5	6	7	8	9	10	11	12
Hours of Sleep												
Weight gain/Lost												

DAILY DEPRESSION TRACKER

13	14	15	16	17	18	19	20	21	22	23	24	25	26	27	28	29	30	31

SADNESS LEVEL

OTHER SYMPTOMS

SLEEP AND WEIGHT

Month: _____ **DAILY DEPRESSION TRACKER**

Day	1	2	3	4	5	6	7	8	9	10	11	12

SADNESS LEVEL

	1	2	3	4	5	6	7	8	9	10	11	12
High												
Medium												
Low												
None												

OTHER SYMPTOMS

	1	2	3	4	5	6	7	8	9	10	11	12
Fatigue												
No appetite												
Overeating												
Repeated thoughts												
Unmotivated												
Lack of Concentration												
Irritable												
Anxiety												
Isolating self from others												
Thoughts of Death-Suicide												
Feeling hopeless												
Feeling worthless												
Indecisive												

SLEEP AND WEIGHT

	1	2	3	4	5	6	7	8	9	10	11	12
Hours of Sleep												
Weight gain/Lost												

DAILY DEPRESSION TRACKER

13	14	15	16	17	18	19	20	21	22	23	24	25	26	27	28	29	30	31

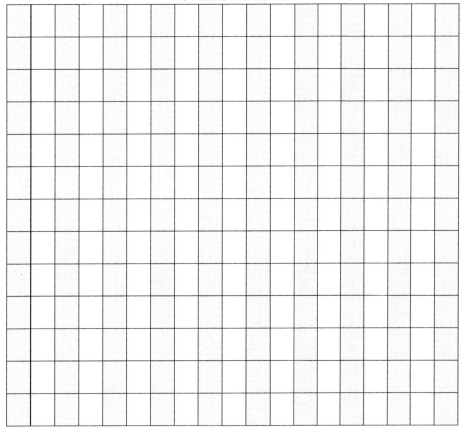

SADNESS LEVEL

OTHER SYMPTOMS

SLEEP AND WEIGHT

Month: _____

DAILY DEPRESSION TRACKER

Day	1	2	3	4	5	6	7	8	9	10	11	12

SADNESS LEVEL

	1	2	3	4	5	6	7	8	9	10	11	12
High												
Medium												
Low												
None												

OTHER SYMPTOMS

	1	2	3	4	5	6	7	8	9	10	11	12
Fatigue												
No appetite												
Overeating												
Repeated thoughts												
Unmotivated												
Lack of Concentration												
Irritable												
Anxiety												
Isolating self from others												
Thoughts of Death-Suicide												
Feeling hopeless												
Feeling worthless												
Indecisive												

SLEEP AND WEIGHT

	1	2	3	4	5	6	7	8	9	10	11	12
Hours of Sleep												
Weight gain/Lost												

DAILY DEPRESSION TRACKER

13	14	15	16	17	18	19	20	21	22	23	24	25	26	27	28	29	30	31

SADNESS LEVEL

OTHER SYMPTOMS

SLEEP AND WEIGHT

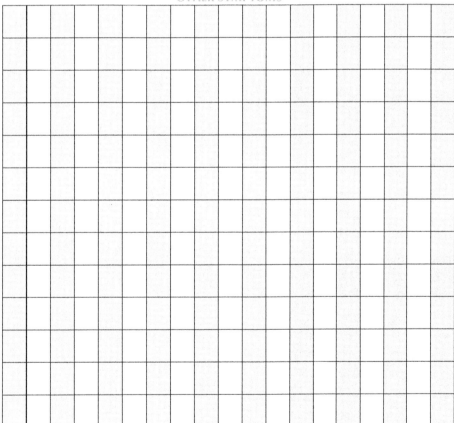

Month: _____ # DAILY DEPRESSION TRACKER

Day	1	2	3	4	5	6	7	8	9	10	11	12

SADNESS LEVEL

	1	2	3	4	5	6	7	8	9	10	11	12
High												
Medium												
Low												
None												

OTHER SYMPTOMS

	1	2	3	4	5	6	7	8	9	10	11	12
Fatigue												
No appetite												
Overeating												
Repeated thoughts												
Unmotivated												
Lack of Concentration												
Irritable												
Anxiety												
Isolating self from others												
Thoughts of Death-Suicide												
Feeling hopeless												
Feeling worthless												
Indecisive												

SLEEP AND WEIGHT

	1	2	3	4	5	6	7	8	9	10	11	12
Hours of Sleep												
Weight gain/Lost												

DAILY DEPRESSION TRACKER

13	14	15	16	17	18	19	20	21	22	23	24	25	26	27	28	29	30	31

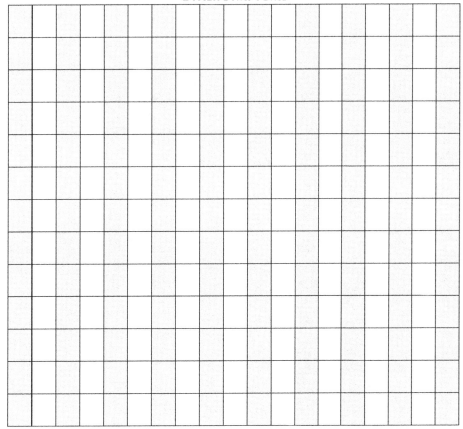

SADNESS LEVEL

OTHER SYMPTOMS

SLEEP AND WEIGHT

Month: _____   **DAILY DEPRESSION TRACKER**

Day	1	2	3	4	5	6	7	8	9	10	11	12

SADNESS LEVEL

	1	2	3	4	5	6	7	8	9	10	11	12
High												
Medium												
Low												
None												

OTHER SYMPTOMS

	1	2	3	4	5	6	7	8	9	10	11	12
Fatigue												
No appetite												
Overeating												
Repeated thoughts												
Unmotivated												
Lack of Concentration												
Irritable												
Anxiety												
Isolating self from others												
Thoughts of Death-Suicide												
Feeling hopeless												
Feeling worthless												
Indecisive												

SLEEP AND WEIGHT

	1	2	3	4	5	6	7	8	9	10	11	12
Hours of Sleep												
Weight gain/Lost												

DAILY DEPRESSION TRACKER

13	14	15	16	17	18	19	20	21	22	23	24	25	26	27	28	29	30	31

SADNESS LEVEL

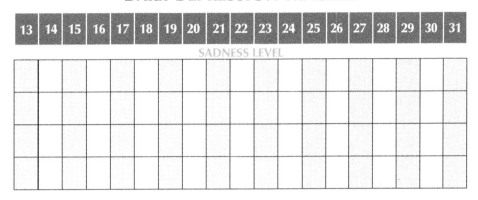

OTHER SYMPTOMS

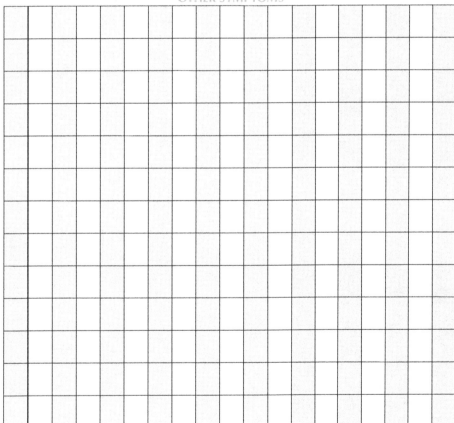

SLEEP AND WEIGHT

Month: _____   **DAILY DEPRESSION TRACKER**

Day	1	2	3	4	5	6	7	8	9	10	11	12

SADNESS LEVEL

	1	2	3	4	5	6	7	8	9	10	11	12
High												
Medium												
Low												
None												

OTHER SYMPTOMS

	1	2	3	4	5	6	7	8	9	10	11	12
Fatigue												
No appetite												
Overeating												
Repeated thoughts												
Unmotivated												
Lack of Concentration												
Irritable												
Anxiety												
Isolating self from others												
Thoughts of Death-Suicide												
Feeling hopeless												
Feeling worthless												
Indecisive												

SLEEP AND WEIGHT

	1	2	3	4	5	6	7	8	9	10	11	12
Hours of Sleep												
Weight gain/Lost												

DAILY DEPRESSION TRACKER

13	14	15	16	17	18	19	20	21	22	23	24	25	26	27	28	29	30	31

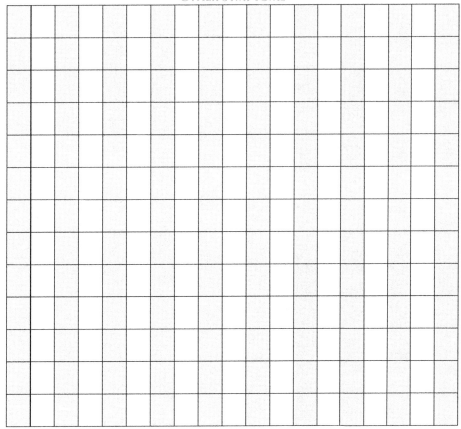

SADNESS LEVEL

OTHER SYMPTOMS

SLEEP AND WEIGHT

Month: _____ **DAILY DEPRESSION TRACKER**

Day	1	2	3	4	5	6	7	8	9	10	11	12

SADNESS LEVEL

	1	2	3	4	5	6	7	8	9	10	11	12
High												
Medium												
Low												
None												

OTHER SYMPTOMS

	1	2	3	4	5	6	7	8	9	10	11	12
Fatigue												
No appetite												
Overeating												
Repeated thoughts												
Unmotivated												
Lack of Concentration												
Irritable												
Anxiety												
Isolating self from others												
Thoughts of Death-Suicide												
Feeling hopeless												
Feeling worthless												
Indecisive												

SLEEP AND WEIGHT

	1	2	3	4	5	6	7	8	9	10	11	12
Hours of Sleep												
Weight gain/Lost												

DAILY DEPRESSION TRACKER

13	14	15	16	17	18	19	20	21	22	23	24	25	26	27	28	29	30	31

SADNESS LEVEL

OTHER SYMPTOMS

SLEEP AND WEIGHT

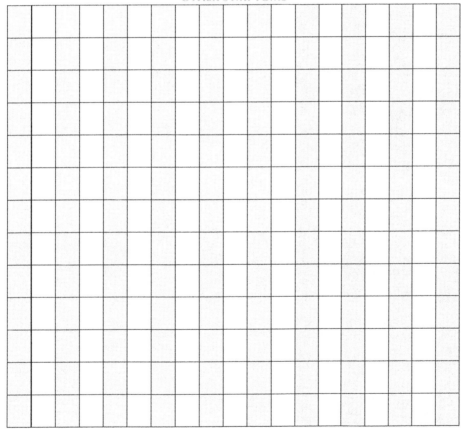

DAILY DEPRESSION TRACKER

Day	1	2	3	4	5	6	7	8	9	10	11	12

SADNESS LEVEL

	1	2	3	4	5	6	7	8	9	10	11	12
High												
Medium												
Low												
None												

OTHER SYMPTOMS

	1	2	3	4	5	6	7	8	9	10	11	12
Fatigue												
No appetite												
Overeating												
Repeated thoughts												
Unmotivated												
Lack of Concentration												
Irritable												
Anxiety												
Isolating self from others												
Thoughts of Death-Suicide												
Feeling hopeless												
Feeling worthless												
Indecisive												

SLEEP AND WEIGHT

	1	2	3	4	5	6	7	8	9	10	11	12
Hours of Sleep												
Weight gain/Lost												

DAILY DEPRESSION TRACKER

13	14	15	16	17	18	19	20	21	22	23	24	25	26	27	28	29	30	31

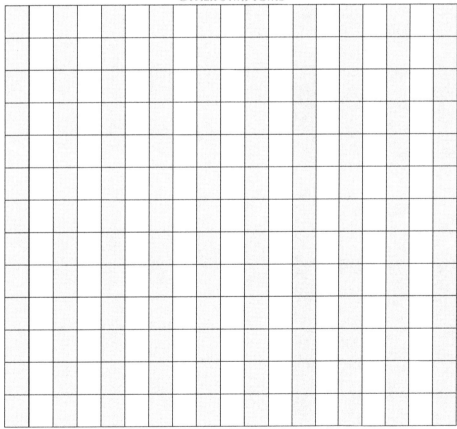

SADNESS LEVEL

OTHER SYMPTOMS

SLEEP AND WEIGHT

Month: _____

DAILY DEPRESSION TRACKER

Day	1	2	3	4	5	6	7	8	9	10	11	12

SADNESS LEVEL

	1	2	3	4	5	6	7	8	9	10	11	12
High												
Medium												
Low												
None												

OTHER SYMPTOMS

	1	2	3	4	5	6	7	8	9	10	11	12
Fatigue												
No appetite												
Overeating												
Repeated thoughts												
Unmotivated												
Lack of Concentration												
Irritable												
Anxiety												
Isolating self from others												
Thoughts of Death-Suicide												
Feeling hopeless												
Feeling worthless												
Indecisive												

SLEEP AND WEIGHT

Hours of Sleep												
Weight gain/Lost												

DAILY DEPRESSION TRACKER

13	14	15	16	17	18	19	20	21	22	23	24	25	26	27	28	29	30	31

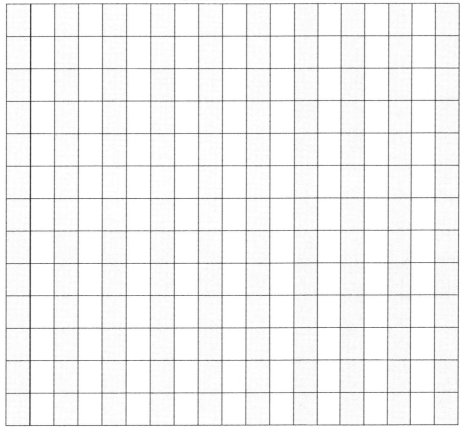

SADNESS LEVEL

OTHER SYMPTOMS

SLEEP AND WEIGHT

Month: _____ **DAILY DEPRESSION TRACKER**

Day	1	2	3	4	5	6	7	8	9	10	11	12

SADNESS LEVEL

	1	2	3	4	5	6	7	8	9	10	11	12
High												
Medium												
Low												
None												

OTHER SYMPTOMS

	1	2	3	4	5	6	7	8	9	10	11	12
Fatigue												
No appetite												
Overeating												
Repeated thoughts												
Unmotivated												
Lack of Concentration												
Irritable												
Anxiety												
Isolating self from others												
Thoughts of Death-Suicide												
Feeling hopeless												
Feeling worthless												
Indecisive												

SLEEP AND WEIGHT

	1	2	3	4	5	6	7	8	9	10	11	12
Hours of Sleep												
Weight gain/Lost												

DAILY DEPRESSION TRACKER

13	14	15	16	17	18	19	20	21	22	23	24	25	26	27	28	29	30	31

SADNESS LEVEL

OTHER SYMPTOMS

SLEEP AND WEIGHT

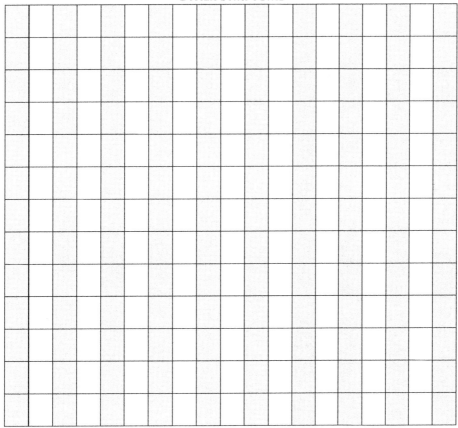

Month: _____ **DAILY DEPRESSION TRACKER**

Day	1	2	3	4	5	6	7	8	9	10	11	12

SADNESS LEVEL

	1	2	3	4	5	6	7	8	9	10	11	12
High												
Medium												
Low												
None												

OTHER SYMPTOMS

	1	2	3	4	5	6	7	8	9	10	11	12
Fatigue												
No appetite												
Overeating												
Repeated thoughts												
Unmotivated												
Lack of Concentration												
Irritable												
Anxiety												
Isolating self from others												
Thoughts of Death-Suicide												
Feeling hopeless												
Feeling worthless												
Indecisive												

SLEEP AND WEIGHT

	1	2	3	4	5	6	7	8	9	10	11	12
Hours of Sleep												
Weight gain/Lost												

DAILY DEPRESSION TRACKER

13	14	15	16	17	18	19	20	21	22	23	24	25	26	27	28	29	30	31

SADNESS LEVEL

OTHER SYMPTOMS

SLEEP AND WEIGHT

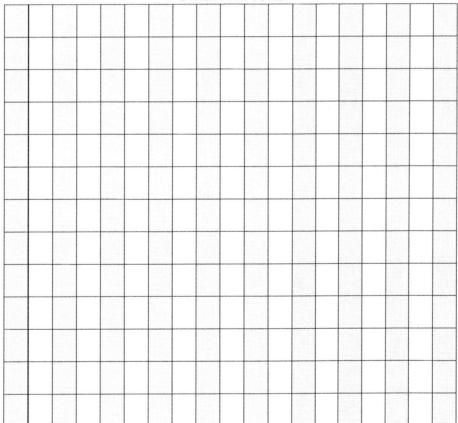

Month: _____ **DAILY DEPRESSION TRACKER**

Day	1	2	3	4	5	6	7	8	9	10	11	12

SADNESS LEVEL

	1	2	3	4	5	6	7	8	9	10	11	12
High												
Medium												
Low												
None												

OTHER SYMPTOMS

	1	2	3	4	5	6	7	8	9	10	11	12
Fatigue												
No appetite												
Overeating												
Repeated thoughts												
Unmotivated												
Lack of Concentration												
Irritable												
Anxiety												
Isolating self from others												
Thoughts of Death-Suicide												
Feeling hopeless												
Feeling worthless												
Indecisive												

SLEEP AND WEIGHT

	1	2	3	4	5	6	7	8	9	10	11	12
Hours of Sleep												
Weight gain/Lost												

DAILY DEPRESSION TRACKER

13	14	15	16	17	18	19	20	21	22	23	24	25	26	27	28	29	30	31

SADNESS LEVEL

OTHER SYMPTOMS

SLEEP AND WEIGHT

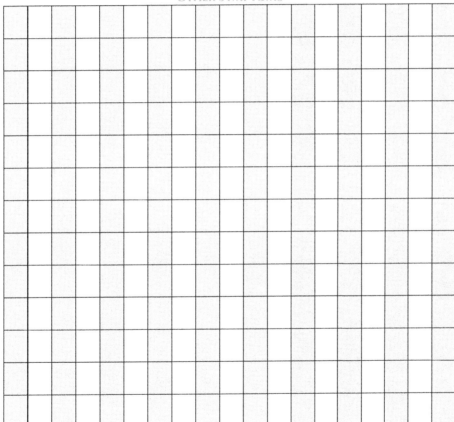

Month: _____ **DAILY DEPRESSION TRACKER**

Day	1	2	3	4	5	6	7	8	9	10	11	12

SADNESS LEVEL

	1	2	3	4	5	6	7	8	9	10	11	12
High												
Medium												
Low												
None												

OTHER SYMPTOMS

	1	2	3	4	5	6	7	8	9	10	11	12
Fatigue												
No appetite												
Overeating												
Repeated thoughts												
Unmotivated												
Lack of Concentration												
Irritable												
Anxiety												
Isolating self from others												
Thoughts of Death-Suicide												
Feeling hopeless												
Feeling worthless												
Indecisive												

SLEEP AND WEIGHT

	1	2	3	4	5	6	7	8	9	10	11	12
Hours of Sleep												
Weight gain/Lost												

DAILY DEPRESSION TRACKER

13	14	15	16	17	18	19	20	21	22	23	24	25	26	27	28	29	30	31

SADNESS LEVEL

OTHER SYMPTOMS

SLEEP AND WEIGHT

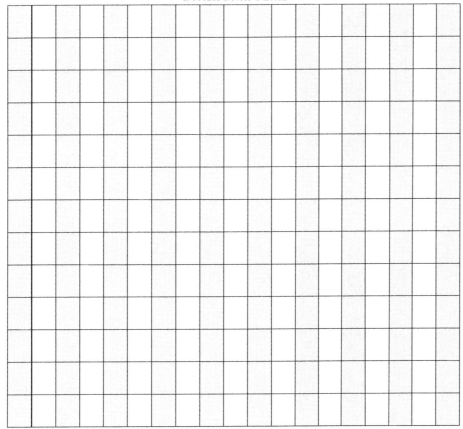

Month: _____   **DAILY DEPRESSION TRACKER**

Day	1	2	3	4	5	6	7	8	9	10	11	12

SADNESS LEVEL

	1	2	3	4	5	6	7	8	9	10	11	12
High												
Medium												
Low												
None												

OTHER SYMPTOMS

	1	2	3	4	5	6	7	8	9	10	11	12
Fatigue												
No appetite												
Overeating												
Repeated thoughts												
Unmotivated												
Lack of Concentration												
Irritable												
Anxiety												
Isolating self from others												
Thoughts of Death-Suicide												
Feeling hopeless												
Feeling worthless												
Indecisive												

SLEEP AND WEIGHT

	1	2	3	4	5	6	7	8	9	10	11	12
Hours of Sleep												
Weight gain/Lost												

DAILY DEPRESSION TRACKER

13	14	15	16	17	18	19	20	21	22	23	24	25	26	27	28	29	30	31

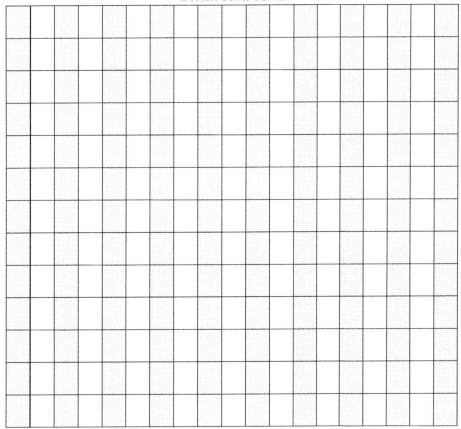

SADNESS LEVEL

OTHER SYMPTOMS

SLEEP AND WEIGHT

Month: _____ **DAILY DEPRESSION TRACKER**

Day	1	2	3	4	5	6	7	8	9	10	11	12

SADNESS LEVEL

	1	2	3	4	5	6	7	8	9	10	11	12
High												
Medium												
Low												
None												

OTHER SYMPTOMS

	1	2	3	4	5	6	7	8	9	10	11	12
Fatigue												
No appetite												
Overeating												
Repeated thoughts												
Unmotivated												
Lack of Concentration												
Irritable												
Anxiety												
Isolating self from others												
Thoughts of Death-Suicide												
Feeling hopeless												
Feeling worthless												
Indecisive												

SLEEP AND WEIGHT

	1	2	3	4	5	6	7	8	9	10	11	12
Hours of Sleep												
Weight gain/Lost												

DAILY DEPRESSION TRACKER

13	14	15	16	17	18	19	20	21	22	23	24	25	26	27	28	29	30	31

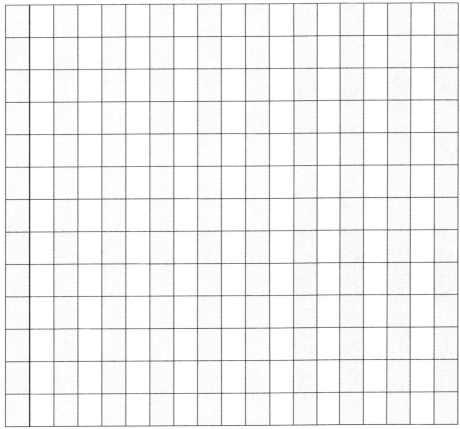

SADNESS LEVEL

OTHER SYMPTOMS

SLEEP AND WEIGHT

Month: _____   **DAILY DEPRESSION TRACKER**

Day	1	2	3	4	5	6	7	8	9	10	11	12

SADNESS LEVEL

	1	2	3	4	5	6	7	8	9	10	11	12
High												
Medium												
Low												
None												

OTHER SYMPTOMS

	1	2	3	4	5	6	7	8	9	10	11	12
Fatigue												
No appetite												
Overeating												
Repeated thoughts												
Unmotivated												
Lack of Concentration												
Irritable												
Anxiety												
Isolating self from others												
Thoughts of Death-Suicide												
Feeling hopeless												
Feeling worthless												
Indecisive												

SLEEP AND WEIGHT

	1	2	3	4	5	6	7	8	9	10	11	12
Hours of Sleep												
Weight gain/Lost												

DAILY DEPRESSION TRACKER

13	14	15	16	17	18	19	20	21	22	23	24	25	26	27	28	29	30	31

SADNESS LEVEL

OTHER SYMPTOMS

SLEEP AND WEIGHT

Made in the USA
Las Vegas, NV
27 August 2021